IMAGES
of America

ETOWAH

The first roads into Etowah were of steel instead of concrete and asphalt. African Americans from Alabama and Mississippi laid much of the original cross ties and rails down, with the help of picks, shovels, dynamite, and mules. An Italian construction crew was brought in to build the Louisville & Nashville (L&N) Dam to supply water for the steam locomotives. Before buildings could be constructed, a 12-foot canal was built to drain the swampy area, and a total of 265,000 cubic yards of red clay was brought in to raise the building site three and a quarter feet in height. Slag from the copper mines of Copper Basin area was brought in for ballast for the tracks. (Author's collection.)

ON THE COVER: The L&N Railroad provided a wide variety of jobs. Road crews, coal firemen, porters, engineers, shop men, and office workers were among many of the diverse skilled workers needed to operate the railroad in Etowah. These jobs also varied greatly in pay scale. On the left is engineer Sid Garwood talking to an unidentified L&N official. In the 1920s, the L&N Railroad employment was over 2,000. At this time, all of Etowah's economy was tied to the railroad industry. (Author's collection.)

IMAGES
of America

ETOWAH

S. Durant Tullock

ARCADIA
PUBLISHING

Published by Arcadia Publishing
Charleston, South Carolina

Library of Congress Control Number: 2013932827

For all general information, please contact Arcadia Publishing:
Telephone 843-853-2070
Fax 843-853-0044
E-mail sales@arcadiapublishing.com
For customer service and orders:
Toll-Free 1-888-313-2665

Visit us on the Internet at www.arcadiapublishing.com

*This book is dedicated to my three sons Brandon, Alex, and Nicholas
Tullock; to Sandra Shaw; and to my friend and father, Doug Tullock.*

CONTENTS

Acknowledgments   6

Introduction   7

1.   In the Beginning   9

2.   Boomtown   15

3.   The L&N Railroad   19

4.   Business and Industry   41

5.   School Days   59

6.   Sports   77

7.   African Americans   87

8.   People, Places, and Things   93

ACKNOWLEDGMENTS

I give my deep appreciation to three past Etowah historians no longer with us. R. Frank McKinney, David Murphy, and Mike Cantrell shared their knowledge of local history with me and many others. A thank-you goes to Bill Akins for sharing his love of local history. Whenever I ask Bill a history question, he always seems to start with Adam and Eve to make sure I understand the background of the story. Thanks go to my history teacher, coach "Red" Barnett, for perking my interest in history and to Kenneth Langley and Clifford Wilson, who are always willing to find answers to my questions with great research.

Thanks also go to the Etowah Historical Commission, the L&N Depot Museum, and the Etowah Arts Commission. I would like to give a special thank-you to Linda Caldwell with the Tennessee Overhill Heritage Association, who pushes me for accuracy and taught me to study the cause of events and their effect on the community. My gratitude also goes to Kathy Taylor, who always seems to know where all the photographs or documents are stored.

A thank-you goes to Sandra Shaw, who encourages me to stay focused to write on paper the information stored in my head so that those who come after me will have an understanding of our heritage. And finally, I want to thank all the individuals who shared their pictures and stories with me for the last 35 years. Together, we can keep Etowah history alive.

All images appear courtesy of the author.

INTRODUCTION

After the Civil War had ended and the end of the nineteenth century approached, there was competition in purchasing many of the short-line railroads in the East. In 1894, Milton Smith of the L&N Railroad and Samuel Spencer of Southern Railroad met and agreed to stay out of each other's way. Together, they decided who would acquire which of the smaller lines. The L&N decided to purchase the former Atlanta, Knoxville & Northern (AK&N) track that went through the Hiwassee River gorge situated near the border of Tennessee and North Carolina.

The steep grade through the gorge made it necessary for the tracks to gain elevation by way of an old "W" switchback until 1898, when L&N civil engineer T.A. Aber designed a rail loop that would allow the train to pass over Bald Mountain without stopping for switchbacks. The L&N loop is the third longest loop in the world and is still in use today carrying passengers from Etowah to Copperhill on excursions from spring until winter.

However, the ruggedness and remoteness of the mountains still caused many problems for the L&N, so in 1902, a new, more direct route from Cincinnati to Atlanta was built. The L&N decided to find a place where the old AK&N and the new line converged to build a facility for crew changes and to service engines. This facility would also serve as the Atlanta Division headquarters and would house workshops, a roundhouse, and manufacturing facilities to make boxcars and repair engines.

After being turned down by landowners near the Hiwassee River and in "Tellico Junction," the L&N was able to purchase 25 acres in a muddy farm area. Civil engineer T.A. Aber designed the first L&N-planned community to meet the needs of the railroad and those who would live there. In 1905, construction workers from surrounding states and Canada were brought in to build the new railroad city. The railroad would influence the culture of Etowah, and that influence is evident 100 years later.

Hundreds of construction workers came to the area from surrounding states to build the L&N shops that ran the length of the newly built town. Entrepreneurs looking to open a business along the new railroad established shops to meet the needs of the workers. As the railroad and the town prospered, the men sent for their families. Dry goods stores, bars, eating establishments, and clothing stores filled the main street of Etowah. The railroad prospered, and along with it, the people who worked here did as well. In just a matter of a few years, the city of Etowah became a bustling town.

Schools were first built in 1915 and expanded from one facility to three in a few years. The Carnegie library was built that same year, providing education opportunities for children and adults.

But along came the Depression of 1929, and the railroad business was slowing down with the rest of the nation's economy. The railroad looked for ways to cut back on costs, and one way to do so was to consolidate resources and labor. The number of divisions of the L&N Railroad was cut in half, and the Etowah offices were moved to Knoxville. In the late 1920s, the railroad was changing the manufacturing of boxcars from wood to metal. The shops in Etowah were making the wooden style, while shops in Knoxville had converted to metal. As a result, the shops in Etowah were closed, and in a period of three years, the shop force shrank from 2,100 employees to 80.

Up to this point, Etowah had been a one-industry town. All the businesses revolved around the railroad and its employees. In 1930, over 100 people filed for bankruptcy. Businesses closed down or relocated to other cities. Local banks failed along with the national economy. The once-thriving railroad was now a shadow of what it once had been.

After nearly a decade of struggling, Etowah reinvented itself by recruiting textile mills. Morgan Manufacturing and Etowah Manufacturing were two cut-and-sew operations that opened up, employing and bringing more women into the workforce. Women workers were vital during World War II. Women and men alike would travel by bus each day to Alcoa for work.

After the war, the economy brightened, and people were encouraged to spend more money to build the economy. The government encouraged people to purchase cars and to travel. Small motels called motor courts were built up and down Highway 411 as the tourist business began to take hold. Motor courts in Etowah built during the early 1950s included the Etowah Motel, Holiday Terrace, Hershey Motor Court, the Dogwood Motel, and the Tennessee Motel. Grocery stores also changed to more self-service supermarkets, like Doug's Supermarket, Galloway's, and K.C. Supermarket.

One of Etowah's most prosperous times was during the mid-1950s. In 1956, Etowah celebrated her 50th birthday with the Golden Jubilee with several weeks of fun and entertainment. The preparation for this time was as fun as the actual events. Men throughout the community grew beards and referred to themselves as the "Brothers of the Brush." If a man did not grow a beard or have an exemption pin, he was fined as a fundraiser for the project. More community spirit was evidenced during this celebration than at any other time in Etowah history.

During the 1960s, several manufacturing companies came to the area, which strengthened the local economy. J.M. Huber and Beaunit Fibers were two of the new companies. A group of citizens lobbied and raised initial funds for a new hospital, and soon Woods Memorial Hospital was built.

By the mid-1960s, a new highway was built to Athens. The new Highway 30 was straighter and corrected the problems with flooding on the old highway. This eased travel to Athens to shop. A new concept of mass merchandising was built just inside the city limits of Athens. Soon people from Etowah would pick up paychecks from work on Friday, go to the bank, and head over to Athens to shop at the new giant store and eat at the new fast food restaurant next door.

More people were now trekking to the county seat for shopping. Businesses with stores in Etowah and Athens now decided that two stores were not needed and closed the one in the smaller town of Etowah. The new highway had a huge impact on the Etowah economy. And in the early 1970s, the new Interstate 75 made it easier to go to Knoxville and Chattanooga for shopping.

By the late 1970s, it was time for Etowah to change course once again. Etowah built an industrial park on the northern border of the city and has recruited several new industries to the area. In 2008, the city renovated the downtown with new bricked sidewalks and vintage light fixtures.

In 2002, the Tennessee Overhill Heritage Association purchased the Old Line Railroad from Copperhill to Etowah. Railroad excursions now take place from April to November on this line carrying passengers through the Cherokee National Forest and over the historic L&N loop. The excursion brings over 10,000 out-of-area visitors to the region and makes the railroad a significant part of Etowah's economy once again.

The L&N depot continues to be the anchor for the downtown area. The depot grounds are the location for most of the community gatherings, and the depot has 43,000 visitors annually. The museum in the depot shares the culture of the railroad and the influence on the people and the lives of those who call Etowah home today.

One

IN THE BEGINNING

Efowah Depot

The first building to be constructed was the passenger depot. A construction crew from Blue Ridge, Georgia, under the leadership of L&N master carpenter Nathan York, constructed the two-story building out of yellow pine. The Victorian-style 15-room building was built with beaded walls and an elaborate staircase. By 1916, the Atlanta Division headquarters had grown so much that an addition was built to provide more office space.

Farmers in the surrounding communities of Carlock, Grady, Cog Hill, Pleasant Grove, Wesleyanna, and Williamsburg came to Etowah in search of extra jobs or full-time work that was more dependable than relying on yearly farm crops. Construction workers were needed to build the shops for the railroad as well as buildings for businesses to accommodate the large population moving in. This c. 1912 photograph is of Tennessee Avenue and Ninth Street facing north.

Although the city of Etowah began in 1906, it did not incorporate until 1909. By then, the business districts of Tennessee Avenue and Ninth Street were full of prospering businesses. The streets were dirt, and after a heavy rain, pedestrians could sink up to their knees in mud. A foot log was placed in front of the depot for access to the businesses. Most of Etowah's businesses were on the west side of Tennessee Avenue. This photograph was taken at Tennessee Avenue and Seventh Street looking south.

As the railroad men moved in, there was a large need for housing. The railroad constructed the YMCA building on Tennessee Avenue between Eleventh and Twelfth Streets. Costing $17,000, this grand wood-and-brick two-story structure was 46 by 80 feet and had a basement with 10-foot ceilings, 66 rooms, steam and electric heat, "complete waterworks," and a slate roof.

Some railroad men worked at the shops and found rooms above businesses. Others who were gone days at a time would get a room at the YMCA when they were in town. For the pleasure and convenience of its occupants, the YMCA had a dining room, tennis courts, pool tables, and checkers tables. The cost of staying there was 25¢. The YMCA was torn down in 1929.

As more wives and families joined their husbands in this new community, many stayed in the boardinghouses that were springing up. Often, wives of railroad men ran boardinghouses. They could make a living while raising a family in the same house. The owner would prepare food for the men and keep their rooms clean. This boardinghouse was owned by A.R. and Gladys Ingram and was located on Tenth Street between Tennessee and Ohio Avenues.

Hotels were built in Etowah's earliest days. The Risk Hotel, built by Coot Smith, was built on the corner of Tennessee Avenue and Eighth Street. Drs. Froneburger and J.O. Nichols soon bought it. The doctors took the names of their daughters Glena and Nora and renamed it the Glenora Hotel. One of Etowah's most unique industries was the Glenora Cigar Company in the back of the building. Owner N.G. Dixon rolled 300 cigars a day. The hotel was torn down in the late 1980s.

Other hotels that also served as boardinghouses include Mountain View Hotel, a large building at Tennessee Avenue and Fifth Street, and the Boxwood Hotel, located a few doors down. The Stafford Hotel was built in 1907 by J.H. Stafford and was located at 624 Tennessee Avenue. It was in operation until about 1970.

Brothers P.A. and L.N. Kinser opened the first drugstore at 708 Tennessee Avenue. Kinser's mixed not only medicine but also Coca-Cola before bottling took over in 1911. In the early days, Dr. L.C. Ogle had an office upstairs and would broadcast the World Series by megaphone to about 2,000 listeners below. The broadcast came in via telegraph through the L&N wires in the depot.

The first post office was located in a shanty next to the railroad tracks. It soon moved to this location at 630 Tennessee Avenue. It then moved one block to 706 Tennessee Avenue before being relocated in 1961 to the corner of Ohio and Ninth Streets. The post office moved once again to its current location at Tennessee Avenue and Fifth Street.

Two

BOOMTOWN

From the beginning in 1906 to the late 1920s, Etowah experienced a large industrial and business explosion along with the influx of people moving to the new frontier. With the assistance of the L&N planners and leadership in town, power and running water soon arrived. Roads and sidewalks were paved, and businesses flourished. News of the success was heard in nearby cities and states, and those looking for work and business opportunities came to Etowah. Several financial institutions like the Bank of Etowah, located at 618 Tennessee Avenue, were opened to fulfill the financial needs of the community.

A key element to Etowah's success was a weekly newspaper, the *Etowah Enterprise*. In 1906, Capt. T.F. Peck started what was one of the longest-running businesses in the community. Peck printed the first newspaper on January 5, 1907, and it became the voice of the community recording events, applauding citizens and civic groups, and serving as critic, cheerleader, and sometimes as an active conscience. Editor R. Frank McKinney established a "Twelve-Point Program" to define the goals of the community. Keeping the goals before the citizens allowed leaders to focus on what was needed to move the town forward. The building on Ohio Avenue was originally a two-story wooden structure.

Supplies for local stores were shipped into Etowah by trains. Railcars packed to the roof would arrive at the freight depot at Ninth Street with dry goods, groceries, sugar, sides of meat, and cottonseed. Everything from clothing to ice cream packed with ice would arrive by train. Workers loaded the goods on wagons and distributed them to the local stores.

In 1911, Etowah had three movie theaters. One of these was the Crescent Movie Theater with continuous moving pictures. The earliest theaters had hand-cranked movies shown with gas lamp projectors in small buildings with rows of wooden chairs. The Crescent Theater was located in the 600 block of Tennessee Avenue.

Fire stoves, usually burning coal, provided heat in the early days. This greatly increased the chance of fires, and Etowah had no organized fire department. In 1913, the first fire department was organized with J.A. Leath, a local funeral director, as chief. Members of the first fire department were Howard Blake, O.W. Wells, Bill McKay, L.C. Elmore, S.D. Hughes, Albert Bayless, Lee Grant, Olin Rogers, Frank Roylston, D.L. Brickey, C.C. McElroy, F.F. Abbott, Preston Fickle, Robert Powell, Henry Williams, and W.C. McKinney. In the early 1920s, the town of Etowah bought a bright new American-LaFrance fire engine and built a new fire station next to the Carnegie library, where it stands today.

Tennessee Avenue was first paved in 1921 at a cost of $25,000. This project was funded by a partnership between the L&N Railroad and the city. This street would eventually become part of the highway system that presented the railroad its stiffest competition. Pictured here is the 700 block of Tennessee Avenue.

An unfortunate part of life created a need for a very important business in Etowah. This was Center and Powell Funeral Home, located on Ohio Avenue and Ninth Street. The early horse-drawn hearse would take loved ones to their final resting place. The funeral home was owned by N.C. Powell and Carl Center.

Three

THE L&N RAILROAD

Jobs were difficult to get in the early 1900s, and working on the railroad was considered a prize job. These jobs were paid in cash on a monthly basis and did not depend on a good crop on the farm. The work was hard, and the hours were long. Conditions were not good, and it could be dangerous work. The toughness of the early railroaders is evident in the faces and character of these men. Pictured here are Roy Dean (left) and Jess Sisson, who worked as trackmen on L&N extra gang no. 4 out of Etowah.

Early rail crews were often made up of men from the same families. One member would get on a crew and would recommend the foreman hire his brothers. Such is the case of the group here, known as the Grant crew. They include Ode Daughtery, Pat Dills, Amos Grant, Bill Grant, Jim Grant, W.J. Grant, Harrison Stiles, and Chin Vaughn.

It was very common for rail crews to work 12 hours a day, seven days a week. The common tools for a rail man were a shovel, sledge hammer, and a bucket. A person who had worked on a rail crew and still had all 10 fingers was considered unusual due to the dangerous work.

Water was important to a rail yard. Water was gravity fed a mile away from the L&N Dam to fill the steam engine, and water from the two water towers at the rail yard was used to power equipment. This picture was taken on Christmas day in 1906, and icicles can be seen descending from the top of the tower.

Although the shops were indoors, it was still difficult working conditions. The winters were extremely cold, and the summers inside the metal-roof buildings would get unbearably hot. Some of the buildings had rough planks thrown up on the side to protect the equipment. There were potbellied stoves in most buildings to provide heat for those standing a few feet from the fire.

There were many moving parts in the railroad shops. Conveyor belts and cutting tools were in constant motion. Oversized wrenches and other heavy tools were used daily to build and repair engines and cars. Accidents were frequent in these conditions.

Denim overalls are always thought to be synonymous with railroad workers. They allowed workers to carry with them the tools needed during the day. Also important was a good hat to help stay warm in the winter and to keep the sun off during the summer. Good shoes helped workers to stand on their feet all day long.

The L&N shops covered the entire distance of the rail yard. Workers provided most of the business in Etowah. The buildings were removed after the closing of the shops in 1931.

Steam coming from engines and from the shops' machinery fills the winter air. In the front left of this picture is the pipe that would swing from one track to the next to fill the steam engines with water. This water was gravity fed from the L&N Dam.

The shops in Blue Ridge were closed down after the shops in Etowah were completed. Many of those working in north Georgia made their way to the Etowah shops to get work.

Etched in the hands and the faces of these men is evidence of a tough working environment. At this time, one could either work for the railroad or work on a farm.

One of the best-paying and most-desirable jobs was locomotive engineer. The 1910 census reveals a diversity of origins of these skilled workers who came to Etowah from Georgia, Kentucky, Missouri, Ohio, and even as far as Canada. Each engineer developed his own whistle sound, and they were as varied as the men's background. Townspeople always knew who was manning the controls by the engineer's signature whistle.

The engine pictured here is on top of the turntable. Engines would drive to the center of this large cog, and the apparatus would rotate 180 degrees to turn the engine in the other direction.

Keeping up with railroad business creates lots of paperwork, which provided a lot of jobs in the depot. Pictured here from left to right are Clarrine Rudder, ? Hale, ? Turleyfield, ? Miller, ? Harris, ? Adams, W.J. Mahoney, and W.R. Ballard.

Workers in this depot office are C. Stoner, G.R. Watkins, Miss Neal, A.A. Moffet, and A.E. Thorton.

C.A. Clayton moved his family from Tate, Georgia, to become the first L&N station agent in Etowah.

The railroad provided a wide variety of jobs as well as a diverse pay scale. The clothing in this picture depicts the difference in pay as well as in job titles. Pictured here are C.A. Clayton, agent; Henry White, porter; Guy Hickey, janitor; Floyd Tanner, office boy; Charles Clayton, ticket clerk; John Melton, porter, and Fred McGhee, clerk.

By 1907, the L&N depot was completed and housed a large number of employees.

Wooden boxcars were manufactured in the L&N rail yard. The surrounding area had an ample supply of wood, which was another reason that made Etowah a good choice for the rail yard. Bill Swann leans against one of the boxcars made in the Etowah rail yard.

Several members of the Garwood family worked as engineers. Some worked the southern route of Etowah to Atlanta while another ran the northern route from Etowah to Corbin, Kentucky. Garwood family members have continued throughout Etowah's history to be business and civic leaders as well as government officials.

Coal was an important part of the railroad business. Much of the early rail business was hauling coal from the mines of Kentucky to the growing industries in Atlanta. Hundreds of coal cars moving daily down the L&N new line were referred to as a "black river of coal." Coal was also used as fuel to power the early steam engines.

Some jobs on the railroad were harder than others. Men would constantly shovel coal into the hot furnaces to keep the steam pressure up to move the train forward. Shoveling coal was not only a hot job but was physically demanding on the back. Brakemen rode on top of moving cars wearing goggles to keep the smoke and cinders out of their eyes. The men could wear a heavy hat but were not allowed to pull it down over their ears.

Some of the men working on the tracks were known as pile drivers. Pile drivers would connect the rail to the cross ties below with large rail spikes. One man would hold the spike while the other would drive the spike into the tie with a sledge hammer. This took a great deal of strength and a lot of trust in one's partner.

Keeping the trains moving smoothly was a difficult job. Constant repairs had to be made quickly. Rock slides, trees falling on the track, and washed out lines are common problems. Papa Allen's bridge crew, seen here, was responsible for repairing the many bridges along the L&N line.

Because of modern-day equipment and regular inspections, rail accidents are not as common now as they were in the earlier days of rail. Tools used in this picture of line repairman P.W. Jones have vastly improved safety. Now, many of the repairs and replacements are done with computers and heavy equipment, although there is still a lot of difficult manual labor along the lines.

In August 1927, a large celebration was held in honor of the safety efforts and the success of the L&N Railroad. L&N officials from around the South came to celebrate with all the employees in Etowah. As reported in the September 1927 edition of the L&N company magazine, there was a barbecue as well as festive music. Congratulatory speeches were made and pictures of all employees were taken. Considered to be one of Etowah's greatest moments, a few years later, this get-together would be forgotten. Pictured are, from left to right, (first row) C.F. Harmon, Joe Powell, G.H. Berry, S.W. Jennings, and Howard Brown; (second row) W.B. Anderson, J.W. Plumley, G.T. Putman, W.H. Ratliff, H.O Miller, and G.B. Smith.

The entire town was dependent on the railroad. Thousands of jobs and hundreds of businesses were all tied to one industry. For years, money had been ample, and the railroad city had enjoyed the successes of the last two decades. Buildings that were quickly built during the early days were replaced with better ones to handle the additional business. Good housing had replaced boardinghouses and railroad shanties. In the late 1920s, it seemed that there could be no end to Etowah's good fortune. But the world has a habit of changing.

In 1930, the railroad suffered a downturn in business. In order for the L&N to survive, consolidations were needed to be made. Duplications of services would need to be eliminated. Much of these services were duplicated in nearby Knoxville, where boxcars were being made from steel instead of wood.

By 1927, 2,100 people were working in the shops and another 250 manned the trains that came in and out of Etowah daily. Line repairmen like the Eaves crew pictured here also worked out of the Etowah location. Included in this crew are Charlie Eaves, William Buckett Moss, Burch Eaves, Will Eaves, Letchee Eaves, and foreman Starling Swanson.

The decision was made to close the shops in Etowah. These buildings were dismantled, and equipment was sent to other shops. The workforce went from 2,100 to 80 in a period of three years. Ninety percent of the men in Etowah were employed by the railroad, and businesses relied on the railroad as well. The lack of diversification crippled Etowah. The lucky ones were transferred, while others were laid off without work. In 1930, the town was left with vacant housing, and 105 bankruptcies were filed.

The exodus of the shops did not completely remove the railroad's influence on the town. Passenger cars still used the depot as a stopping point until 1968, when passenger service was discontinued.

Passenger service still brought business to the community. Passengers would get off the train and get a bite and some reading material in the Grab-all Room of the depot.

Etowah's population had decreased from 4,209 in 1930 to 3,362 in 1940. The sound of the shop whistle would no longer cut through the air to summon workers. Etowah would encounter some tough years but would eventually emerge with a more diverse economy.

The sound of a steam engine would also exit as new technology arrived. These changes made the trains more efficient, requiring less manpower.

In 1945.Engineer Fred Stewart on diesel No. 458
which pulled through Knoxville from Atlanta.

In 1945, Fred Stewart brought the first diesel train No. 458 through Etowah on the way from Atlanta to Knoxville. "Like driving a T-Model and a Cadillac," said Stewart of the difference between the old steam engine and the new diesel. Stewart was a 35-year L&N trainman.

Four

BUSINESS AND INDUSTRY

After the initial businesses came in to accommodate the building of the new city and the railroad, word got out in the outlying region of the business opportunities in the growing town. Higher-quality clothing stores, grocery stores, and supply houses filled the west side of Tennessee Avenue. Ninth Street was also filled with new vendors. Stores opened tabs for rail workers to pay at the first of the month when paychecks came in. Etowah business had a prosperous beginning. Here a standing line over a block long awaits the grand opening of First National Bank in 1908 at 720 Tennessee Avenue.

McKinney's Department Store was the third store opened in Etowah. Originally opened in 1906 at 600 Tennessee Avenue by Sam McKinney, prosperous business led him to expand in 1910, moving the location to 726 Tennessee Avenue. McKinney's continued to grow in the 1920s, moving to the 800 block of Tennessee Avenue.

Many modern-day clothing stores cater to women, but Etowah's early population was more male than female. This store had a large inventory of hats, umbrellas, and shoes for the men. Many clerks were available to assure quality customer service.

Several grocery stores had rolling stores. Grocers had routes in and out of the city, where they would drive their horse-drawn wagons taking orders one day and delivering the groceries the next. Jake Shamblin of the Grady community, Robert Miller at west Fifth Street, and Oscar Mashburn were some of the earliest rolling stores in the area. Pictured here is a rolling store owned by H.P. Armstrong.

Customers did not gather their own groceries. They would hand the grocer their list or tell them what they wanted, and the grocer would then gather the goods for the sale. Some grocers would then deliver the groceries to the home. Pictured in Reed Bros. Store are, from left to right, Mance McGhee, Toots Burgin, Horace Curtis, Oran Reed, and Nell Reed.

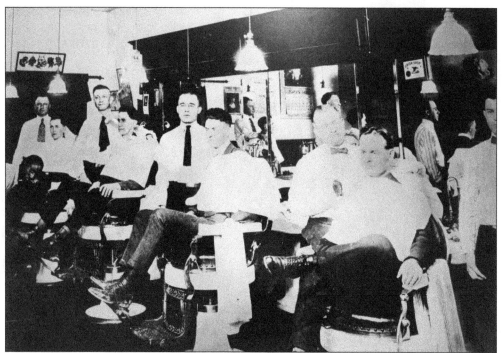

T.T. Rogers opened the first and largest barbershop in Etowah. An advertisement in 1907 listed him as a "Tonsorial Artist." Rogers provided other services as well, like having clothing pressed while patrons enjoyed their showers. Afterwards, customers could get a haircut and shoe shine. Rogers was located at 728 Tennessee Avenue.

R.E. Stone was the owner of Ninth Street Barbershop, located on the corner of Ohio Avenue. Barbershops were a great place to catch up on the local news.

In 1912, N.C. Powell and Carl Center opened Center and Powell Hardware and Furniture Store. Their slogan was "Marry the girl and we'll furnish the home." The store was located at 810 Tennessee Avenue. In 1933, Powell moved his store after Center's death to 824 Tennessee Avenue.

Brothers Luke and Bill Powell along with brother-in-law Ray Sloop continued the store operations after their father's death. Before the big-box chains arrived in the mid-1960s, stores kept large inventories with a wide variety. Powell's was one of the more popular stores in town.

A group of investors opened Peoples Bank, located at 900 Tennessee Avenue in 1910. In 1920, T.W. Cantrell sold his farm on Mecca Pike to buy a controlling interest. This was the beginning of the Cantrell family business enterprises. Peoples Bank merged with First National Bank in 1930 following the Depression.

First National Bank opened in 1908 at 720 Tennessee Avenue. After merging with Peoples Bank in 1930, First National closed its doors in 1931. Because banks were not federally protected, hundreds of locals lost all the money they had in the bank at the time. This was another crucial blow with the closing of the railroad that same year.

White's Shoe Shop was on the corner of Ninth Street and Ohio Avenue. Men from the railroad shops would spend all day on their feet and wore the store's shoes. They would bring them to Jim White for repairs and new soles instead of buying new shoes.

Johnson's Department Store is Etowah's oldest continuous-running business. E.L. Johnson opened the clothing store in April 1938. After his death, his wife, Mattie, continued the business. Yale Webb came to work for Mattie Johnson in 1962, and he purchased the business in 1974. Johnson's continued under Yale's leadership until his death in 1989. The store is currently owned by Yale's son Don and continues to bear the Johnson name. Johnson's is known for quality clothing and beautiful window displays.

Early drugstores had soda fountains and sandwich shops. These made popular hangouts for the high school kids. Gem Drugstore, located at 700 Tennessee Avenue, was located next door to the Gem Theater. Locals would stop by before and after the movie for a quick bite to eat.

Donald Rule's Drugstore, located at 820 Tennessee Avenue, was always packed with customers and merchandise. Rule's was known for great hamburgers and coke floats and for his disorganized way of displaying his goods. He was famous for saying, "I know I have it here if I can just find it." Pictured from left to right are Lena Dixon Rule, Donald Rule, and an unidentified assistant.

Tallent Drugstore at 718 Tennessee Avenue had a soda shop and also served as the bus stop in Etowah. Bruce Tallent purchased the store in 1923 from O.A. Rule who had a confectionery store. In 1946, Brown Alsip bought the business and continued until his death.

Cafés and restaurants adorned the downtown streets of Etowah throughout the years. Messer's Hole in the Wall Café was located at 628 Tennessee Avenue.

S.W. Cannon opened Cannon's Café in 1946 at 614 Tennessee Avenue. With soldiers coming home from World War II, businesses were experiencing new growth.

As World War II ended, people were encouraged to enjoy their new prosperity by purchasing new cars and traveling. Etowah had five car dealerships at one time, including Rocket Motors at 119 Ninth Street. Pictured here are owners Paul Cantrell (left) and Sam Watters in 1954.

Early entrepreneurs learned to adapt to changes in business needs. Numerous individuals owned multiple businesses at different times. An example is W.I. Benson. Benson ran a transfer company during the late 1920s and into the 1930s. There were many people moving in and around the community at this time and then out of the area after the closing of the railroad shops. In the late 1930s, Benson opened a taxi service.

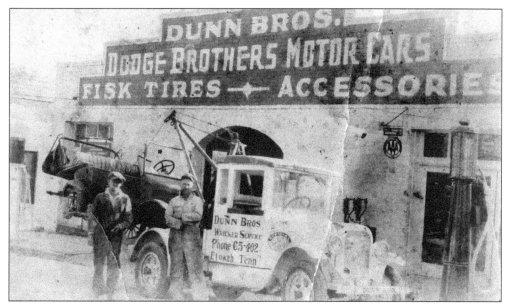

The Dunn family is another that made adjustments in business over the decades. This family was involved in a variety of businesses including the Etowah Coal and Ice Company, Dunn and Cockrell Hardware, B&E Restaurant, Chilhowee Steak House, Cash Hardware, Dunn Livery Stable and Feed Store, King Dunn's One Stop Store, Sabo Restaurant, Shepard and Dunn Insurance, the Country Store, Tom Thumb Restaurant, and Boe Peep Ice Cream Shop. Seen here is Dunn Bros. Wrecker Service and Garage.

Modern technology was changing after 1950, and so were businesses in Etowah. With the new popularity of television, stores began selling the latest models. Radio and television repair shops opened to meet demands. Lyndus Harper (left), owner of Harper's Furniture store, shows the latest model to Paul "Red" Sitzlar.

Business owners went to great lengths to bring in customers. One promotion, which was considered the greatest sale in Etowah, occurred in 1915 at the business of Reed Bros. Department Store. John and Oran Reed carried Buster Brown Shoes, which was the most popular brand of shoes for many decades. The Buster Brown Shoe Company of St. Louis, Missouri, had hired a four-foot, two-inch 22-year-old man to portray the character Buster Brown along with his dog Tige. The Reeds brought Buster to their store to the delight of all the customers seen here awaiting his arrival.

Although most businesses are now on Tennessee Avenue, Ninth Street was booming during the early years. This picture shows two successful businesses on Ninth Street in 1908. Pictured is the first location of Reed Brothers along with W.J. Samples Home Furnishings.

This picture was taken following the widening and repaving of Tennessee Avenue in 1947. The Lions Club purchased streetlights from Fifth Street to Ninth Street for a cost of $4,600.

This 1941 photograph shows a mixture of old and new times. There are horse and buggies parked alongside cars. The streets do not have stripes, so drivers went on whatever side of the road was convenient.

Murphy's Funeral Home was located at the corner of Eighth Street and Ohio Avenue. Murphy's later merged with Jewell Weber's Ambulance Service. Weber joked that if the funeral home business were down, he would just slow down his ambulances.

The early 1960s was a prosperous time in Etowah. New county schools were being built at the same time Etowah was building a full-service hospital. J.M. Huber and Beaunit Fibers were industries that had replaced the railroad and added to the list of textile industries in the area. The Martin Theatre showed current motion pictures weekly. The theater was originally built in 1917, renovated and enlarged in 1927, and continued as a movie theater until the 1970s.

Tennessee Ave. looking south
Etowah, Tenn.   P-28

The Martin Theatre was originally named the Gem Theatre. In December 1948, its name was changed to honor partner Roy Martin, who was killed in a plane crash in February 1948. In 1960, the movie A *Dog of Flanders* was the first to be shown in the theater in color.

The East Tennessee Telephone Company, seen here in 1910, was located above the Etowah Bank & Trust Company at 618 Tennessee Avenue. Operators transferred phone calls in the upstairs portion of the building for nearly 40 years.

Five

SCHOOL DAYS

When the L&N Railroad planned Etowah in 1902, educational facilities were part of the design of the town. At first, there were mainly men in the town, but they soon brought in their families, and others moved in as well. It did not take long to see the need for a school system. In 1915, the first public school building was erected on the corner of Fifth Street and Pennsylvania Avenue. Before 1915, there were several schools located in people's homes with limited children attending. The first school building was Etowah Grammar School (EGS). It originally consisted of one building, seen on the right of this photograph. The second building was not added until 1922. A gymnasium and cafeteria was added in later years. When EGS was first built, it housed grades one through eight until 1921, when more facilities were needed for this growing community. Etowah Grammar School closed in 1972 when a new school was built following a fire at the junior high school two blocks away. EGS was used for a community center until the turn of the century. The last remnants of Etowah Grammar School were torn down in 2012.

Children filled the air with laughter playing on the monkey bars. This Head Start class taught by Nancy Gentry Cochran (far left) included Chris Farmer, Martha March, Durant Tullock, and Tina Cloonan.

A small building was located in the back of the playground where Lena Tye taught piano lessons.

Music was an
important part of the
culture in Etowah and
began at an early age.
Music and instruments
were easily accessible
because of the railroad.
Railroad employees
and their families
could get free passes
to go to Knoxville
or Atlanta on the
weekend to find the
latest music available.

This photograph includes future principal Matney Reed and teacher Fannie Mae Mayfield.
Pictured are, from left to right, (first row) Ross Mulkey, Phillip Jarvis, two unidentified, Doug Jones,
Audrey Watters, Tom Saffles, and unidentified; (second row, in no particular order) Elizabeth
Johnston, I. Jarvis, Ruby Ledburn, and Doris Stone Brown; (third row) unidentified, Harry Long,
Betty Garwood, unidentified, Katherine Long, two unidentified, Carl Anderson, Matney Reed,
and ? Wilson; (fourth row) F.C. Stokes, Hilda Campbell, unidentified, teacher Clara McCombs,
Adrienne Haren, Joe Adams, and unidentified.

Pictured are, from left to right, (first row) Bunk Whittaker, Earl Carmichael, William Denham, Bill Todd, three unidentified, and Joseph Marshall; (second row) Irene Epperson, Johnnie Bob Brown, two unidentified, Hazel Clayton, Inez Hopper, three unidentified, and Elizabeth Barnett; (third row) unidentified, Ozell Whittaker, Elizabeth Moore, Katherine Williams, Mary Nell Stewart, unidentified, and Jean Adams; (fourth row, in no particular order) Janie Burgin, Augusta Bridges, Evelyn Shinlever, and Sam H. Saffles; (fifth and sixth rows, in no particular order) G.B. Smith, Tom Pendley, Malcolm Howland, and Stella Peck.

Among the students pictured here are W.A. Wilson, Ed Ingram, E.M. Akins, Jack Stalcup, Lester Reynolds, Thomas ?, Imogene Flowers, Louise Young Keith, Charles McDonald, Edna Rogers, Lillian Nelson, Ed Ingram, Elma Frances Holsclaw, Mary McKinney, Margaret McConkey, Nell Corin, Lucille Edison, Ruth Upshaw, Mahalia Burrow, Lawrence Hicks, Fronie Brackett, Mabel Casteel, Myrtle Swartout, John Yarborough, Carl Forrester, and ? Teague.

There were several regional schools around the outlying areas of Etowah. One of these was North Etowah School. Pictured in 1935 in no particular order are Alidean Ashley, Frances Elliott, Orene Puett, Bobbie Williams, Mary Ella Tullock, Mary Liner, Janice Brown, Mary Elizabeth Miller, C.V. Standridge, Raymond Ferguson, Ben Calhoun, Emma Lou Harris, Edna Watson, Boyd Bivens, George Watts, Broughton Chastain, and Elmer Harris.

Pictured in Thelma Keith's 1922 class are, from left to right, (first row) Lucille McHaney, Margaret McConkey, two unidentified, Lucille Edison, Corine Patterson, Imogene Melton, Minnie Lou Snyder, Mary McKinney, Vivian Latham, Edna Rogers, and Lillian Nelson; (second row) Louise Pardue, unidentified, Nell Caughron, four unidentified, Madralia Burila, Ruth Upshaw, Ed Ingram, unidentified, Lewis Young Keith, Carl Forrester, and Jean Stalcup; (third row) Pauline Rouse, Ed Harris, Grant Melton, unidentified, Harold Ledford, W.A. Wilson, unidentified, Harold Delay, unidentified, and Lorene Parsons; (fourth row) unidentified, Ray Tallent, unidentified, Edward Beavers, and Thelma Keith.

This 1951 kindergarten class includes Chris Whittle, Karen Whittle, Elaine Baker Colson, Burke Garwood, Bill Robinson, and Chuck Alverson.

Ruth Brown was a first-grade teacher in this 1957 picture. From left to right are (first row) Nancy Anderson, Patricia Hembree, Dennis Best, Billie Ray Freeman, Teresa Gravely, Johnny Green, and Kathy Jenkins; (second row) Ray Harrill, Gary Coleman, Gary Garwood, Joyce Arms Farley, James Wallace Hopper, Corkey Gaston, Mike Cockrell, and Joyce Hoffman; (third row) Diana Burnett, Jeanne Johnston, Max Calhoun, Linda Beavers, Gene Cheek, Jackie Cline, and David Wilson; (fourth row) Janice Armstrong, Carloyn Hood, Sheila Davis, Tim Carter, Jimmy Casteel, Mack Harwood, Tom Epperson, and unidentified.

The students performed plays and operettas each year. Parents would get patterns to make each costume. Pictured are, from left to right, (first row) Jeff Lovelace, Steve Hughes, Gene Bull, Brad Duckett, and Dan March; (second row) David Watson, Winky Groover, and Jimmy Clark. This picture was taken in the early 1960s.

Before the days of computers and keyboards there were chalkboards and erasers. Good penmanship was also stressed in classes. Pictured in Billie Ingram's second-grade class are Butch Jones, Dexter Key, Tony Melton, Roger Murphy, Margaret Reed, Lawrence Rucker, Mike Scoggins, Skillet Smith, Dewayne Sutton, Audrey Trotter, Tony White, and Marlene York.

Etowah first began high school classes in the Carnegie library building on Ohio Avenue. The first classes began around 1917. Etowah's education needs continued to grow, and a new high school was built in 1921.

Etowah High School was completed in 1921 on Eighth Street at the present site of the Etowah City School. This high school was in operation until 1966 when Englewood and Etowah merged to form the county school of McMinn Central. Englewood and Etowah were big rivals in sports, and the merging was a big adjustment for the students.

Etowah Junior High School was completed in 1923 and was built by the citizens of the community. This facility was in operation until 1972, when it was destroyed by fire.

This picture of Etowah High School majorettes was taken at the Etowah High School in 1945.

The Rexall Drugstore was the place to take a date after the eighth-grade prom. Pictured here from left to right around 1949 are Della Francis Sutton, Margaret Sutton, Jimmy Williams, Austin Shadden, Spencer McClary, and two unidentified students.

Members of the 1935–1936 Sub-Deb Club include, from left to right, (first row, sitting) Temple Stewart, Mary Dunn, Tommy Shephard, Mary Abbott, and Ruth Tootsie Walls; (second row, standing) Johnnie Bob Brown, Jean Adams, Bertha Dean Upshaw, Elizabeth Moore, Mary Spencer, and Helen Sloop.

Taken in 1954, this band picture includes Cissy Gaston Joines, Jim Bull, Linford Bull, Ed Bates, and Carol Durant Tullock.

The 1936 picture of the major and majorette corps was taken on the steps of the Carnegie library.

Spreading the spirit for the Etowah High School teams in the late 1950s are Phyllis Bivens, Wanda Harris, Linda Lattimore Cheek, Brenda Mincey Watts, and Nancy Shearer.

Fire drills always presented a great break from the regular routine of class. This picture was taken at the east side of the Etowah Junior High School.

Basketball banquets in the 1950s were held in the Etowah Junior High School gymnasium.

The 1958 Happy Days kindergarten class included Jeannie Brown, Chris Carter, ? Cheek, Mrs. Duffy, Stanley Dunkle, Tommy Harwood, Layne Hoffman, Jane Ivins, Steve James, Wes James, Butch Jones, Gene Jones, Carol Morgan, Roger Murphy, and Marcus Simpson.

Etowah Grammar School teachers in 1969–1970 included, from left to right, (first row) principal Matney Reed, unidentified, Dorothy Brown Stinson, Anna Harris, Norma Dickey, Mrs. Bill Huddleston, and unidentified; (second row) Fannie Mae Mayfield, Billie Ingram, Kathleen Watson, Mildred Abbott, Averal Dodd, Eddie Stansel, Sue Webb, Ethel Bowers, Juanita Gentry, Ruth Isibill, and Louise Wilson.

In the late 1950s to early 1960s, Helen Hopper taught in classrooms that were cooled by ceiling fans and warmed by radiator heat.

Kenneth "Skinny" Green was principal of Etowah Junior High School during the 1950s.

To protect the safety of students crossing the road, Etowah Junior High School formed a safety patrol. Led by principal Eldon Pack, the patrol consisted of Ford Clayton, Glenn Curtis, Elmo Green, Gene Jarvis, and Ross Mulkey.

Taking care of the nutritional needs of the students are the Etowah High cooks. All meals were prepared fresh and cooked on site.

Students in Helen Hopper's 1956–1957 class included James Armstrong, Johnny Austin, Dennis Bain, Robert Ball, Billy Benson, Curtis Benson, Edward Berry, Marilyn Bowers Coe, Georgia Bridges, Earl Carmichael, Gary Carroll, Beverly Centers, Helen Chambers Rudder, Roger Cockrell, Jerry Collins, Elizabeth Crumley, Hedy Dale, Jerry Daugherty, Linda Jo Deal, Joyce Derrick, Joy Faye Farmer, Nancy Ferguson, Richard George, Billy Hampton, Jane Haney, David Hankins, Jerry Hill, Lynn Holt, Gary Johnson, and Steve Keeton.

Pearl Walker taught seventh grade at Etowah Junior High School. Students in her 1956–1957 class included Charles Maney, David Mantooth, Harold Martin, Hilda Martin, Tina Martin, Gail Metcalf, Wanda Moore, Tim Newberry, James Parrott, Bobby Patton, Carol Pickett, Darrell Pickett, Rachel Quam, Betty Rogers, Butch Rose, Louis Rouse, Susie Sloop, Jean Stewart, Joyce Stinson, Gloria Tallent, Linda Teague, Glenda Thompson, Raymond Wilson, Barry Woods, Larry Yarber, and Faye Zimmerman.

After the fire in 1972, the Etowah Grammar School and Etowah Junior High School merged to form the Etowah City School. Students went for a short time to North Etowah Baptist Church while the new Etowah City School building was being completed. The building was later burned to the ground for safety reasons.

Six

SPORTS

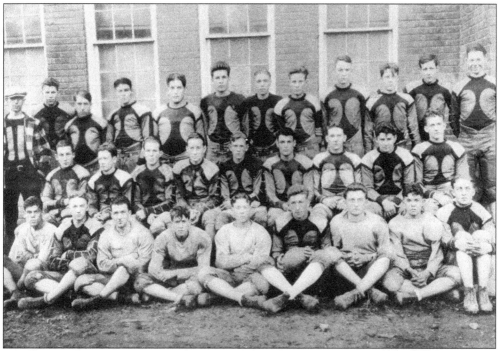

When men arrived in 1906 to work for the railroad, there was a need for recreation. The town was full of bars and pool halls for distractions, but during the spring and summer months, outdoor sports became the popular pastime. Ball teams made up of the workers would play against teams from nearby towns. With the arrival of public schools in the early 1920s, ball teams were part of the school activities. Tom Saffells went on to play professional baseball for the Pittsburgh Pirates and Kansas City Athletics from 1949–1955. Walter Claude "Steel Arm" Dickey played for the Negro League in the early 1920s. Youth leagues and school sporting programs continue to be an important part of the community today. Pictured here is the 1926 Etowah High School football team.

The 1921 Etowah baseball team was made up of railroad men. The team included, from left to right, (first row) Paul Howell, Hobo Clark, W.D. Thompson, J. King Dunn, Paul Richards, J.P. Carlock, and George Cochran; (second row) Dorie H. Mcghee, W.A. Carlock, A.E. Stacey Adams, Glenn M. Swanson, Bill Lyons, Sam Saffells, and Richard Roberson.

In 1928, the baseball teams played in a sandlot near the YMCA building. In later years, ball fields were built next to the high school at Eighth Street and others on Sixth Street.

Etowah High School sports included basketball, football, baseball, and in earlier days, tennis. Etowah had a tennis club in the 1930s in Todds Park, which was located in the south end of Etowah. Pictured here is Etowah High baseball player Doug Tullock.

The early football teams played without face guards on their helmets and little or no padding. Without the extra protection, injuries were common.

The high school field pictured here next to the high school was not prepped the way fields are today. According to former football player Doug Tullock, "The lot was full of gravels and was hard clay covered with just a little grass. When you hit the ground, you knew it was going to hurt." This was the 1948–1949 football team.

The 1951 Etowah High School football team included, from left to right, (first row) Bill Bates, Jimmy Williams, Dewey Truelove, Tom Aderhold, Billy Webber, Doug Tullock, Jimmy Watson, and Booney Lewis; (second row) J. Wilson, Mike Cantrell, Duly Sisson, Roy Stone, Eddie Williams, Ray Stone, Charlie McConnel, and Bill Battle; (third row) Paul Walker, Don Pangle, Ray Clendenen, Bob Webb, Kenneth Gregory, Charlie Robinson, and Dave Alloway. Some of the coaches during the 1940s–1950s included Hobert "Feets" Jones, Wes Barker, and Elmer Baker.

Coaches in the final days of Etowah High School included, from left to right, assistant coach Claude Catron, head coach Virgil Stalens, and assistant Bob Lambert.

The 1944 Etowah High School basketball team members are, from left to right, (first row) Joe McClain; (second row) Jack Fox, Bob Harper, coach E.K. Baker, Don Marion, and Bob Kinnamon; (third row) Wayne Frazier, Bob McKay, Bill Haskins, Jerald Roberts, Woody Kinnamon, and Jess Barclay.

The 1947 EHS basketball team included, from left to right, (first row) Bob Kinnamon, Wallace Clendenen, Bob Harper, Loly Simmonds, and Hoyt Roberson; (second row) Joe Moates, Jim Tom Carson, W.A. King, coach E.K. Baker, Charles Blaylock, Jim Pangle, and Ted Painter.

Seating at the high school gym was on one side of the court with a balcony surrounding the gym. This picture was taken in 1948.

Etowah High School opened its doors in 1921, and this 1922 picture shows a well-dressed basketball team. This was during some of Etowah's most prosperous days. Holding the ball is Darrell Rule.

Girls got into basketball in the early days of Etowah history, too. Included in this picture are Marjorie Bivens, Dorothy Brown Stinson, Jean Delaney, Don Edwards, Frances Hampton, Betty Harris, Helen Dean Harris, Inez Johnson, Emily Kincaid, Elizabeth Long, Nellie Mann, Margaret Madsen, Creed McClure, Betty Painter, and Helen Webb.

The 1958–1959 Etowah Junior High School basketball team members are, from left to right, (first row) coach Kenneth Gren, Elaine Baker Colson, Brenda Faye Smith, Linda Sisson, Judy Martin, Judy Brown, and Janet Davis; (second row) Barbara Kellar, Carol Cole, Katherine Curtis, Mary Nell Deal, Patsy Weber, Mac Roe Snyder, and Brenda Moore.

This Etowah Junior High School team included, from left to right, (first row) unidentified and ? Hill; (second row) Leonard Ingram, Ronnie Carroll, Larry Jenkins, Don Newman, and Jerry Fain; (third row) Jake Cantrell, Shad Newman, Jimmy Morris, Jimmy Robinson, and Danny Conner.

This Etowah Junior High School girls' basketball team is practicing outdoors.

Until 1964, not only were the schools segregated, but also the ball teams. Pictured here is an early Parkstown School football team.

Seven

AFRICAN AMERICANS

The first settlers in what is now known as Etowah were African Americans. African Americans originally owned the land bought for the rail yards, as well as property bordering Eighth Street from Tennessee Avenue to Louisiana Avenue. During the railroad strike in 1922, black men from Alabama and Georgia were brought in as strike breakers. Segregation that existed in the South also existed in Etowah. It was evident in work, living areas, recreation, and schools. The early struggles strengthened the relationships in family, churches, and community, and this strength is evident today. The Charlie Kincaid family was one of the families that endured many struggles. Charlie lost his job when he "came out on strike." Charlie later found work as a waiter in the Glenora Hotel to support his family. Family members included Charlie, Elizabeth, Della, Margaret, and Lucille. Lucille later became a weekly columnist in the *Etowah Enterprise*.

George Boyd was the only African American in Etowah to serve in World War I. He was a member of the Company L Infantry that was stationed in Etowah. George worked various jobs including working as a waiter in the Glenora Hotel and in T.T. Rogers' barbershop. Boyd is also credited with digging the canal system by hand from Tennessee Avenue to Pennsylvania Avenue.

Minus Moss was a member of a hardworking family. Several members of his family worked for the railroad. Minus went to work as a cook at the YMCA.

Schools were segregated until the 1960s. Black students went to Parkstown School, East Etowah, or West School. High school students were bused to Athens to attend Cook High School. Pictured here are students from Parkstown School.

This picture was taken at the East Etowah School around 1930. Pictured are, from left to right, (first row) Dave Samuel, Claude Hitchcock, Howard Jackson, Percy Taylor, Frank Stovall, Henry Brown, Frank Brown, Ed Mooney, Calloway McDermott, Cornelius Brown, Dan Jerdan, Dan Williams, Jack Williams, and Pearl Taylor; (second row) Lawrence Gellespie, Holly Wally, Elizabeth Jackson, two unidentified, Gertrude Williams, Pauline Williams, unidentified, Catherine Taylor, Manie Taylor, Elizabeth Carter, Azalee Taylor, Edith Parris, Geneva Parris, Geneva Jackson, Sheridan Carter, and Willie Mae Stovall; (third row) Charles McDermott, Rachel Mooney, Lolita Mooney, unidentified, Henrietta McDermott, Marie McDermott, Geneva Ervin, Zenova Errkin, Osborne McDermott, Amos Jackson, John T. Parris, two unidentified, and T.G. Parris; (fourth row) Elsie Mooney, Leslie Wiley, Maxine Lowry, ? McDermott, Ida Stovall, Lacie Mae Jerdan, Neecie Jerdan, Maxine Hitchcock, Nathaniel Wiley, Floyd Dickey, Alfred Parris, Chester Gellespie, Homer Brown, ? Carter, Abraham McDermott, Sam Gellespie, and ? Brown. Teachers in the window are Susie Mae Tate and Mr. Resinour.

This bus, pictured in 1929, would take students to Cook High School 10 miles away. The roads at this time were not paved and could be hazardous.

Several years later, the county provided better transportation. Students would be bused to Cook High School until the late 1960s.

The church was a place for social gatherings and family time as well as a place to worship. Mount Olive AME Zion in Parkstown and Star Bethel Church in East Etowah are two places of worship that have served the community for decades.

Eight

PEOPLE, PLACES, AND THINGS

L & N Depot, Etowah, Tenn. P-30

In a community of 3,800 people, most people know not only their neighbors but also most of the people in town. Buildings like the depot, library, schools, and churches create the foundations that build and bind the town. Etowah holds many annual events like the Fourth of July celebration, fall arts-and-crafts festivals, and Easter egg hunts, which bring the community together. Etowah had its first community event in 1924 and has continued every year since then. This chapter will share the people, places, and things that are the heartbeat of Etowah.

The L&N gazebo was built in 1931 in memory of August McClary Jr., who was the son of a local businessman. Eight-year-old August died in a drowning accident a year earlier. The gazebo was originally built as a bandstand and did not have the upper portion of the building added until a later date. In 1964, windows were added to the structure, and the gazebo served as the office of the Etowah Chamber of Commerce until 1977, when it was restored along with the depot. At that time, the windows were removed

Located in the L&N depot lawn, this structure is a monument built in 1922 to commemorate the fallen soldiers from Etowah in World War I.

The National Youth Administration built the Etowah Scout Lodge, located on Pennsylvania Avenue, in 1938. The NYA was a program created after the Depression to give students a job to help them be able to go to college.

The L&N depot was built as the first public building in Etowah in 1906. In 1912, the Portico Room was added to what is now the front of the depot. In the mid-1970s, the depot was in bad need of repair. Because the building was no longer in use by the railroad, plans were made to tear it down. A group of citizens, spear-headed by city finance director Edith Burgess, believed that the building was a focal point in the community and needed to be saved. In 1977, the railroad sold the building and the grounds to the city for $35,000, and the group raised $200,000 to remodel the building. Today, the L&N depot houses a railroad museum and several offices. The depot is also the boarding site for the Hiwassee River Rail Excursions, which provides passengers a trip on the Old Line to Copperhill, Tennessee.

Lloyd Campbell was the project leader for the building of the Etowah Scout Lodge. Lloyd also was in charge of the construction of another building on the same lot that was originally planned for a workshop to build furniture for the local schools. The building instead was used as the National Guard armory due to World War II.

Troop No. 74 is one of the oldest-continuing Boy Scout troops in the nation. The troop was formed in 1927 and has had strong leadership over the years. Some of the leaders include Dr. Boyd McClary, Fred McGee, Lloyd Campbell, Gene Witt, Leroy Hershey, Steve Dunkle, Tom Strickland, Dennis Underdown, and many others. Some of the scouts in this picture, taken around 1945, include Ralph Grubb, Joe Allen McClain, and Delbert Puett.

The scouting program developed many future leaders like Leroy Hershey (center). Leroy joined scouting around 1949 and remained as a scout and a leader until his death in 2012. This Eagle Scout later served as a community leader in civic organizations and government positions and was a business leader. Hershey received many honors for his commitment to scouting and his community including the Silver Beaver Scouting Award, Volunteer of the Year Award, and Etowah's highest honor, the Cornerstone Award, which is given to the few who have made lifelong commitments to the community.

The Etowah Scout Lodge served Boys Scouts, Girl Scouts, Cub Scouts, and Brownies, like the group seen here in the late 1950s. Included in this picture are Ann Dunn, Patricia Cooper, Katherine Ann Baker, Chris Carter, Marcie Guegold, Jane Ivins, Margaret Reed, Audrey Trotter, Connie Akins, Marlene York, Pat Simonds, and several unidentified Brownies.

This 1968 Cub Scout pack includes, from left to right, (first row) Randy Watts, Dennis Johnson, Scott Shearer, David Willis, Jimmy Richardson, John Sharp, Dana Martin, Kim Martin, Danny McDonald, Durant Tullock, and Charlie Bernhard; (second row) Brian Calfee, unidentified, Jimmy Worley, Wayne Martin, Vic Wyatt, Tony Self, Bart Blackwell, and Scott Thompson; (third row) Terry Dills, unidentified, Pete Witt, Greg Jones, Michael Tullock, Jimmy Walker, Terry Huddleston, Kennard Kyle, Scott Shamblin, and Dale Perkins; (fourth row) Bill Huddleston, Peggy Watts, Joann Worley, Lorene Walker, unidentified, Barbara McDonald, Stephanna Blackwell, and Bill Collins.

A variety of music from classical to bluegrass has filled the air in Etowah. Pictured in his new band uniform is Charlie Rule. Charlie became a second-generation business owner operating Rule Furniture.

Dick Dickson Palmer taught classical music in Etowah. Before 1930, classical instruments were commonly seen in Etowah. Seen here around 1926 is the Dick Palmer Orchestra.

The first Etowah Community Band was formed in 1924. Included in the photograph is Capt. David Lillard.

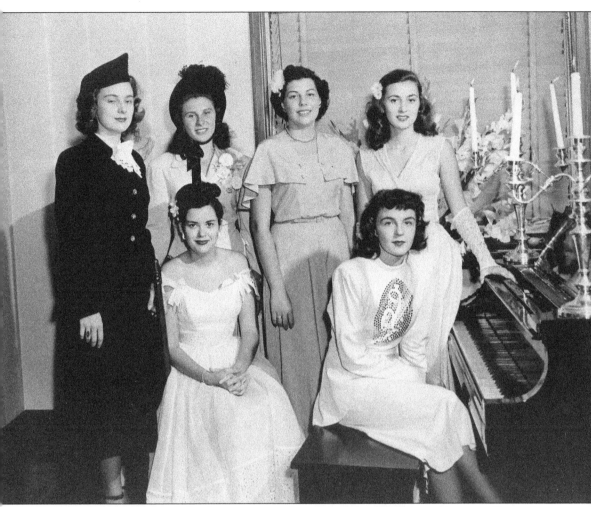

Piano recitals were not only for the enjoyment of music but also served as social events. Pictured are, from left to right, (first row) Mintie Cantrell Willson and Mary Tom Cantrell; (second row) Myrtle Dawson Wheeler, Nancy Cantrell Dender, unidentified, and Carol Cantrell.

N.B. White Head (left) and Clyde Runion performed around the Etowah area combining the classic sound of the violin with guitar.

The Gem Theater ceased showing movies in the early 1970s. Jake Tullock returned from performing with bluegrass legends Flatt and Scruggs to start the Starr Mountain Jamboree as a weekly performance in the Gem Theater for several years. The Starr Mountain Jamboree had a variety of guests and regulars. One of the guests was future star Crystal Gayle. Some of the regular performers included in this picture are, from left to right, Sid Keane, Larry Fain, three unidentified, Mack McKinney, Beth Keane, and unidentified.

Jake Tullock, known onstage as "Cousin Jake," was a member of bluegrass legends Flatt and Scruggs and the Foggy Mountain Boys for 25 years. Jake performed with many well-known performers, including Bill Monroe and Marty Stuart. Cousin Jake was part of the comedy duo of Cousin Jake and Uncle Josh performing for thousands of people throughout the world. Flatt and Scruggs were regular performers at the Grand Ole Opry and played venues like Carnegie Hall in New York. Jake later retired to his home of Etowah and worked with the Etowah police dispatcher. Jake continued to entertain locals with his comedy and his trained dog, Smokey Lady. Tullock began his career of entertainment with the Tullock Singers. The Tullock Singers would travel to homes, schools, and churches to share their talent. In 1940, the Tullock Singers won a contest and got to sing on a nationally broadcast radio station. Jake Tullock is pictured above (center) with Earl Scruggs and Lester Flatt, and at left with his sisters (from left to right) Lillian, Mary Ella, and Dorothy.

Etowah was home to a large unit of the National Guard in the early 1900s. Pictured here are members of the Etowah Council No. 155 Junior Order United American Mechanics.

The home of the 117th L Infantry was the National Guard armory located at the southwest corner of Ohio Avenue and Ninth Street. This picture was taken on the steps of Etowah Carnegie library in 1914. The library was completed in 1915.

During Word War II, the L&N depot and Carnegie library were used by the Red Cross for soldiers fighting in the war. The depot saw many troops embark and return by train. Red Cross volunteers, seen here, include Mrs. H.L. Belt, Mrs. G.H. Berry, Edith Burgess, Emma Cox, Mrs. George Daily, Mrs. T.D. Duncan, Mrs. L.J. Elrod, Helen Ivins, Mrs. Arlie Knox, Mrs. James Lewis, Norma Lewis, Pearl Long, Susie McJunkin, Bertha Ownbey, Mrs. George Painter, Mrs. Jack Parkinson, Mrs. W.L. Schenk, Margaret Sewell, Dora Tharp, and Mrs. Lee Ware.

When Woods Memorial Hospital opened its doors in 1964, a group of local citizens formed a volunteer auxiliary. The women were known as "pink ladies" because of the color of their uniforms. The auxiliary is still serving the community 50 years later.

On of Etowah's biggest legends was Burkett Ivins. Ivins served in many political offices and in law enforcement agencies, including the IRS, as a marshal and as McMinn County sheriff, during the 1920s. Ivins's motto during the 1928 election for sheriff was: "Efficiency, Economy, and Law Enforcement without Violence." According to court records and newspaper accounts, Ivins killed eight men in "self defense."

As a law enforcement officer for the IRS, it was Ivins's duty to confiscate and destroy any whiskey stills. Ivins was vigilant in searching for and destroying these illegal moonshine stills. However, Ivins was also known to be a bootlegger, and by destroying the stills of others, he was putting his competition out of business. This picture was taken after he and his deputies seized an illegal still. Included in this photograph with Ivins (right foreground) are Arthur "Idod" Blair (fifth from left) and Kelly Shoemaker (far left). Ivins later killed Shoemaker.

Ivins was killed in 1947 while awaiting a second trial for the killing of Charles Dunn. His car exploded while backing out of his garage. This murder made national news and was featured in *Time* magazine. No one was arrested for his murder.

Law officers standing in front of the police department building, located at Eighth Street and Tennessee Avenue, are, from left to right, Bob Richardson, Jewell Weber, Carl Moore, Clyde Dale, Bill James, Ernest Barefield, Winston Guy, and city recorder Dan Ivins.

Pictured in front of the Etowah City Recorder's Office are, from left to right, (first row) Easly Miller, Clyde Dale, and Winston Guy; (second row) Reed Morgan, unidentified, Wayne Quinn, and Ida Bivens.

Early firemen seen in this photograph include Bob Deal, Bob Edison, Sam Ellis, Garnin Farris, Fred Lillard, Bill Murphy, Boone Powell, Boe Rudder, Darrell Rule, and Bill Snyder.

Fire department members pictured here include Jewell Weber, Paul Quirk, Donald Perkins, E.C. Williams, Paul Sitzlar, Hubert "Tub" Stone, and Don Bowman.

The Cantrell family members were some of the original settlers in Etowah. The original family lived in the community of Williamsburg and Cantrell Crossroads before Etowah was built in 1906. They are the descendants of revolutionary soldier Tom Cantrell, who is buried in Williamsburg Cemetery. Some members of the Cantrell family went into banking, while others opened other businesses, including the Etowah Lumber Company. Pictured here are, from left to right, (first row) Frank Cantrell, Jim Cantrell, Kate Cantrell, Florence Lockhart, and Jack Cantrell; (second row) Tom Cantrell, Paul Cantrell, and Margaret Marsh.

The O.A. Rule family opened its first business in 1906 and eventually opened 23 businesses in Etowah. The Rules had at least one store open for a consecutive 100 years. Pictured from left to right are O.A., Alice, Donald, Darrell, Edna, and Ruby.

Doug and Carol Tullock began their business career in 1973 after purchasing the Boe Peep Dairy Barn. In 1974, they converted their antique store to a discount grocery store called the Bargain Barn. The Bargain Barn/United Grocery Outlet has grown to 35 stores in five states under the leadership of their son Michael Tullock. Doug Tullock was awarded the Businessperson of the Year Award and the Cornerstone Award, Etowah's highest honor given to those who have given lifelong service to the community.

Hugh Manning opened the Gem Theatre in Etowah. Originally opened as a small theater in 1917, Manning undertook a large expansion in 1927 and invested in a $75,000 renovation. Manning, along with partner Roy Martin, owned a chain of theaters throughout the South but made Etowah his home.

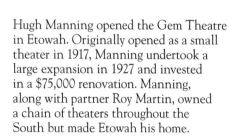

Davis swimming pool located in West Etowah on Fifth Street opened in 1933. An underground stream, which had cool temperatures, fed the swimming pool. The pool closed around 1963. Pictured around 1949 are Red Cross swimming class instructors. They are, from left to right, (first row) Clarence Walker, Bobby Jean Poore, Polly Ellen Webb, and Bobby Cantrell; (second row) Buck Hall, David Murphy, Joyce Anderson, and Nancy Dender; (third row) Annette Hoskins, Johnny Puett, and unidentified; (fourth row) Bill Dender and three unidentified instructors.

When Thomas Upshaw decided to add a second story to his house at 931 Georgia Avenue, he decided to add the first indoor bathtub in an Etowah home. Before then, men would go to the barbershop or the YMCA to take a bath.

Wesley Memorial United Methodist Church was the first church built in Etowah, in 1906. It was originally built on the southeast corner of Tenth Street and Ohio Avenue until a new building was constructed across the street. Wesley was originally called Methodist Episcopal South Church.

This picture is of the second building occupied by the First Baptist Church in Etowah. This large brick structure replaced the original wooden structure. In the 1970s, this structure was torn down to make room for an expanded church.

Pictured here is the men's Sunday school class at First Baptist Church in the late 1920s. Before the rail yards left in 1930, the population of men was much greater. Most men in the community attended a church.

Seen in this picture is the First Baptist Church youth choir.

The original North Etowah Baptist Church was located on Georgia Avenue a few blocks from where it is today. The adults in this picture, taken in 1925, are dressed in their finest church attire. Note the group of boys in the window behind the adults; a closer look will reveal that two of the boys are fighting.

116

Seen here in 1954 is the First Christian Church youth choir and adult choir.

In the early 1950s, Helen Hopper organized a square dance group called "The Sugar Footers." The square dance craze took off, and soon the entire community was dancing to the square dance caller. So many people participated that dances were held in the junior high school gym. In the center of this 1959 photograph are dancers Doug and Carol Tullock.

Teacher Helen Hopper introduced square dancing to the youth at the Etowah Grammar School. She called the group of youngsters the "Sugar Babes." Helen Hopper continued to teach the youth square dancing until her retirement in the 1980s. Some of the dancers in this picture include Robert Sewell, Doug Rule, Kim Guegold, James Wallace Hopper, Jeanne Johnston, Tom Reed, and Bill Landreth.

This group of Sugar Babes went to Etowah Junior High School in 1959. Pictured are, from left to right, (first row) Mary Lynn Thompson, Chris Whittle, Kay Rule, Mickey Witt, Karen Wear, Larry Jenkins, Harriett Sewell, Paul Barnett, Phyllis Patterson, and Leonard Ingram; (second row) Sandra Mills, Paul Wilson, Janice Watson, Billy Robinson, Sandra Green, Bobby Delay, Janet Elrod, David McNabb, Shirley Amos, Don Newman, Susan Leslie, and David Simpson.

The L&N depot lawn has always been the gathering place for most events. This picture from 1961 shows a group of people in front of the gazebo enjoying some music.

The Etowah Utilities prepared the streets for the Christmas parade with the newly purchased Christmas decorations. Parades have always been a part of the Christmas season in Etowah. This photograph was taken in front of Sewell Chevrolet.

Pictured here is one of Etowah's earlier
parades, in 1919. The first car appeared
in Etowah in 1917. By 1925, Etowah
had 781 cars. Pictures from 1915 show
that the earlier parades consisted
of mainly horses and wagons.

The Etowah Band dressed up as
Indians for this celebration in 1930.

The 1956 Golden Jubilee was considered to be the greatest year in Etowah history. Etowah celebrated its 50-year anniversary with a month-long celebration. Business was prospering 10 years after the war, and community spirit was at an all time high. The Golden Jubilee parade had thousands of people involved. The beauties pictured on this float are Joan Brow, Bobbie Mason, Barbara Watts, Ema Rose Williams, and ? Quirk.

Community leaders wore costumes representing the different periods of Etowah history. Shown here are R.J. Harris, Goldman Frase, Hubert "Tub" Stone, and Foosey Cox.

The Golden Jubilee featured a variety of events, including dances, plays, skits, contests, games, and much more. Pictured here are Dennis Wade, Foosey Cox, Gaylord Daugherty, Johnny Witt, and P.L. Amos.

The Brothers of the Brush were very popular during the Jubilee. Every man in town was required to grow a beard or buy an exemption pin that he had to wear throughout the event or pay a fine. Money from the fines went to finance the events. The men had a beard-growing contest to see who could grow the best beard and the biggest beard. Pictured here are Dennis Wade, John Witt, R.J. Harris, P.L. Amos, John Paul Alley, Roy Anderson, Gaylord Daughtery, Sam Sims, Matney Reed Foosey Cox, and Clyde Lewis.

Another fundraiser for the jubilee was the makeshift jail on the depot lawn. If a man was caught without a beard or his exemption pin, he was put in the stockade until he paid his fine. Among those pictured here are Gaylord Daughtery, Red Trotter, Roy Stone, Scott Green, and Joe Aderhold.

Thousands of people lined the streets to enjoy the parade. Bands were brought in from around the state. Gov. Frank Clement spoke to the crowd on the depot lawn. After the parade, the crowd enjoyed the amusement park set up in the L&N Park.

Here, Sandy Johnston and Jimmy Bussart enjoy a ride in the Golden Jubilee parade.

The blizzard of 1993 will always be remembered as one of the biggest events in Etowah history. A total of 27 inches of snow fell on the city, leaving power out for days—and in some cases for an entire week.

In 1993, when snowfall was close to two feet, the National Guard used all-terrain vehicles to help get people to warm shelters. Pictured here is the Etowah Scout Lodge covered in snow days after it fell. The snow remained on the ground for several weeks.

Visit us at
arcadiapublishing.com

CPSIA information can be obtained
at www.ICGtesting.com
Printed in the USA
BVHW011118270221
601214BV00008B/14

9 781531 668068